matchbox girl

rachel sandene

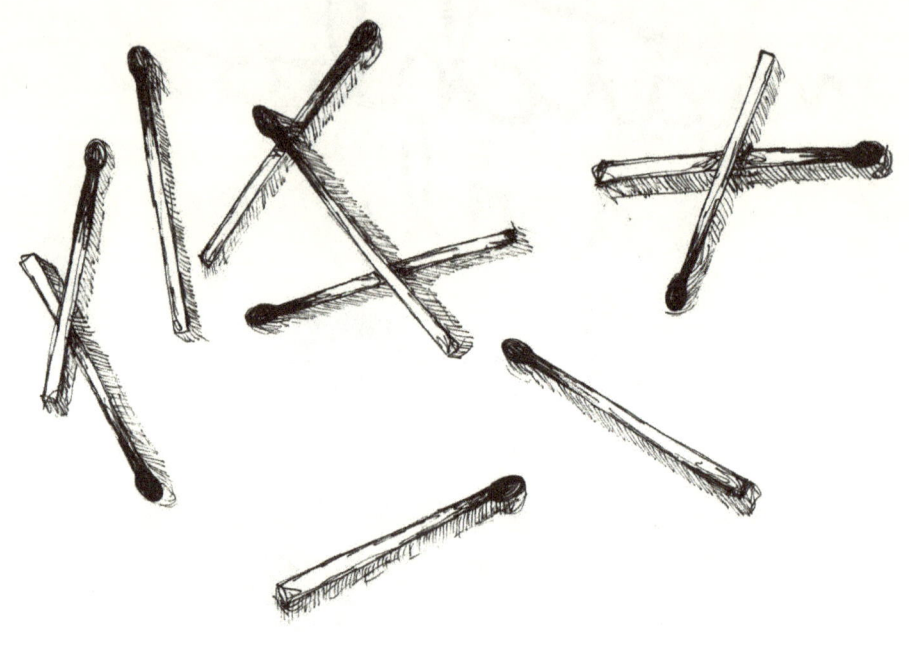

Copyright © 2016 by Rachel Sandene

All rights reserved. This book or any portion thereof may not be reproduced or used in any manner whatsoever without the express written permission of the publisher except for the use of brief quotations in a book review or scholarly journal.

First Edition 2016
ISBN 978-0-692-45750-4

Rachel Sandene: Creativist
3916 Edgestone Drive
Plano, TX 75093

For Matchbox Girls
With smoke alarms in their hearts and
Lighter fluid in their veins and a penchant
For setting themselves on fire
And falling in love.

For Thomas
Together, we played with fire;
We were beautiful while we burned.

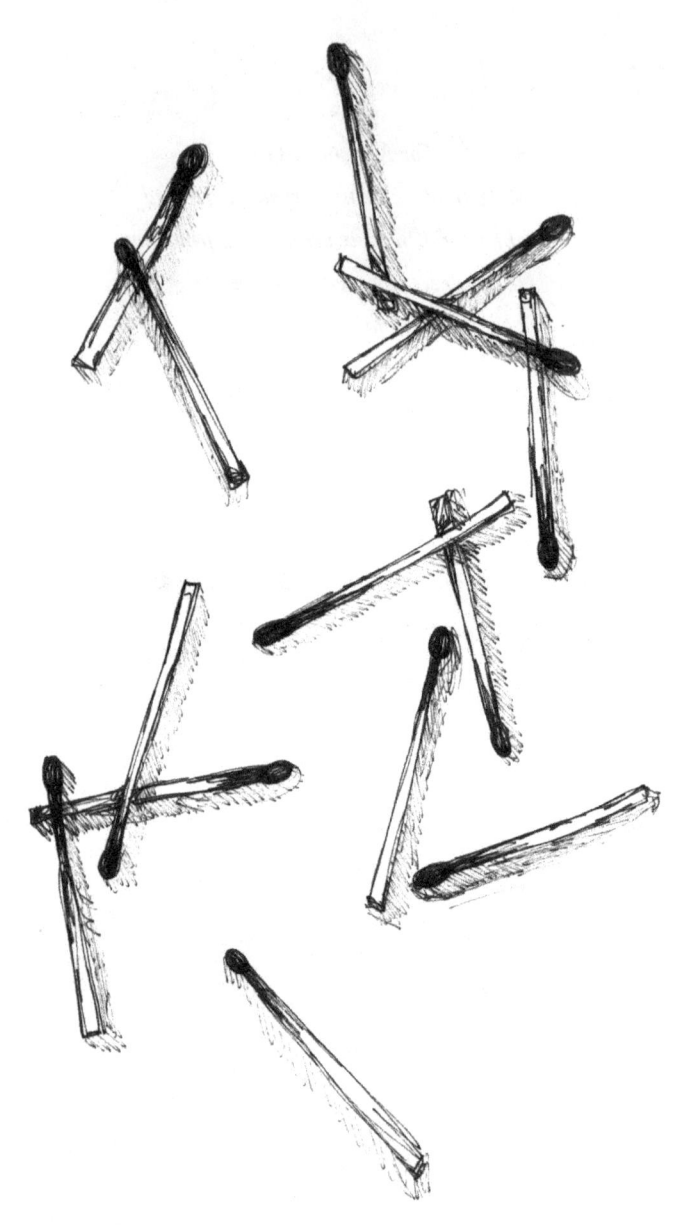

contents

#1: Matchbox girls are highly flammable.   1

#2: Matchbox girls are the ones who get hurt.   23

#3: Matchbox girls rise from their ashes.   43

Index   76

Acknowledgments   78

About the Author   79

#1

matchbox girls are highly flammable.

forever was written on the walls of your mother's kitchen

It starts like this, with the thought that
I wouldn't mind being here forever,
In your mother's kitchen, alone with you.
You're standing a few feet away from me,
Close enough to pull me closer, but instead
You're flipping through the songs on your mother's iPod
And skipping every other one because
They're not Springsteen. You're talking to me.
You're too far away. I can't hear a thing.

I want to ask you to just let it play so I can
Ask you to dance before our chances
Run out. I want to ask you, can we go to your room,
The one with the baby-blue walls and the
Too-small bed and the shelves full of
Springsteen records. I want to tell you how much
I want to stay here, loving you.

But instead we're standing in your mother's kitchen,
Me, leaning against the counter, wishing I could ask you
To dance with me, you, still too distracted
To see all the forevers written on the walls.

It starts like this, with a hope that this moment
Will never end.

It all starts like this, with a longing for a forever
I never wanted to believe in
Until now.

hurricane red

There's a storm front coming through but
I'm not quite sure you're ready. I'm not sure
You know what you're getting yourself into.
I don't know if you'll make it out in time so
I am asking you to leave, now,
Before it's too late.

If you're looking for a pretty love,
You've come to the wrong place.
I am named after disaster, after
Tornado sirens sounding shrill in my bones.
I am named after flashing crimson lights
Telling you to stop before someone gets hurt.
I am spitting out blood, splintered love,
Lightning like cracked teeth. Thunder
Like fractured heartbeats.

Before you start chasing this storm, you should know
The only love I have to offer you is the kind
That will flash-flood your heart, and there will be
No warning. Storms like me don't tell boys like you
When you'll be broken down; boys like you
Don't listen when you are told to run as fast as you can.

There's a perfect storm brewing in my eyes and
I wish you would just look away;
I'm not quite sure I'm ready.
I think it's already too late.

sharp-toothed love

My love has sharp teeth and instincts
That taught it how to hunt.
My love makes friends with wolves and
Keeps their howls locked up in my chest.
My love is dangerous. My love is broken glass.
My love has jagged corners and rough edges
That you'll need more than just your strong hands to smooth.
You'll say goodnight and wake up to find that
I've sharpened my edges again.
My love will cut you open.

My love knows how to sink its canines into prey, how to
Tear it to shreds, how to let the blood dry and leave stains
Beneath my fingernails. My love knows how to kill
A perfectly good thing. My love knows how to wrap itself
Around the throat of a lover, choke him
Until he's gasping for breath, then let go. My love knows
How to let you go, only to pull others closer.
My love knows how to love in all the wrong ways.
I learned the hard way that loving isn't easy and that
When I love, I love too hard.

My love has no table manners;
It will rip your heart out with its bare hands
So many times that you'll stop noticing
When your heartbeat is gone.
My love will snap your spine in two,
Hold you in its jaws until you go limp.
My love will chew you up and spit out your bones.
My love is feral. My love has sharp teeth.

My love doesn't know when to stop.

wild thing

Come out and dance with me, the monster, the beast,
The girl with the razor-toothed grin.
Join this waltz for two, this hunt in three-quarters time;
You'll never understand how feral my love can be,
But you'll love it anyway.
I don't care about you, but I do,
I do, so watch how I dance beneath the full moon:
With a howl in my chest and four legs, ready to run.

I call myself half-human, half-beast. I call myself wild thing.
I call myself broken-boned creature in the dead of night;
You call yourself loaded gun.

racing hearts

The sun is setting, a shade of red I can't quite put my finger on,
But you'll still see it in the shadows of your bedroom after I leave.
It's an almost-summer night and the air is sticky with heat and
Our hearts are probably beating too fast for our own good, but
I don't care. You're by my side and your hand is in mine and
That's all I need. I know it's a bad idea, falling for you like this,
But not all street races end in flames. See, I don't know what to call
This love but it has my pulse pounding in my skull and blood pumping
Through your veins; I hope you'll stay.

I'm chasing after you; you're dragging me headfirst into something
I can't quite explain. All I know is it feels better than being alone.
It's an adrenaline rush, our two hearts racing, our feet hitting
Hot pavement. Our chests are hardly enough to hold what we feel and
You're lying so near to me you can feel I'm out of breath and
Our mouths are too close for words to be necessary;
We're on the road to destruction but it doesn't feel like it's enough.

We're going two hundred down a street called love and maybe
It's a little too much, but I never promised you this love was safe.
I never said it would be easy. I never said we'd make it out alive.
I said I loved you recklessly, breathlessly, from the
Butterfly wings in my stomach to my sweet-tasting lips.
I said I know I'm hard to love but if you just wait long enough,
I'll ignite a wildfire in your veins.

I said my love for you fills my gasoline heart. I said I'm a girl
Who doesn't know how to put out a flame;

I hope you'll stay.

matchbox girl

This is what happens when you light the fuse
Of a girl with gunpowder in-between her teeth.
This is what you get when you try to play with fire.
I'm just looking for an excuse to burn and
You look like you'll give me plenty of reasons.
I hope you came prepared.

Gasoline doesn't mix well with a heart like mine;
I thought I warned you not to come any closer.

Don't make me burn this place down, don't make me
Strike a match on my ribcage,
Don't make me turn my collarbones into tinder.
I am flammable; ask me to make a list of everything
I have ever set on fire and I will return with
A stack of paper and a lighter.
I'll burn it, too.
It'll burn with you.

I dare you:
Come closer.

icarus falling

Our love happened here, somewhere too close to the sun,
Somewhere too high above the ground to think straight.
It felt like Icarus falling. It didn't hurt quite as much
As I thought it would. It felt like your hands in my hair and
The wind in my face. It didn't feel like my bones were breaking;
It felt like something changed.

I've never been scared of heights but I have always
Feared the fall and yet you taught me how to fly without
Looking down. You gave me wings, wax and feathers and
Hollow bones. You gave me the sky
And I took your heart for my own.

Now, with sunburnt skin and molten wings,
You show me that love is nothing to fear.

Now, descending somewhere between water and sky,
I let myself fall.

Now, as we collide with the crashing waves, I learn
Icarus wasn't afraid when he flew too close to the sun;
He wanted to fall into the sea all along.

love poems written in braille

I only know how to love with my heart wide open and
My eyes sewn shut; I am blind. I can't see a damn thing.
So let's play pretend that the stars are just love poems
Written in Braille. Let's imagine that the constellations
Have their own language of love that neither of us know.
Let's make-believe that if you guide my hands towards the sky,
I might be able to tell you what they are saying.
I can't make any promises that their words won't be my own.

This is what the stars say: I love you even though
I've been preparing for the end since the universe began.
I love you even though I don't believe in forevers and infinity
Has never made sense. I love you despite being blind.
I love you because I am blind. I love you because I've said so
So many times and yet every time I still have to shut my eyes tight
So no light can get in.

I've been in the dark for so long I've forgotten what it's like
To see the stars; just tell me we'll make it. Tell me
This won't end again. Guide my hands towards you so
I can read your body like love poems written in Braille.
Bring my fingertips to your lips; show me infinities
I can finally believe in.

This is what the stars say: I'll love you to the end
Of the universe and back if you can prove to me
That the universe has no end.

So let's play pretend that maybe we'll last forever. Let's imagine
That maybe infinity will finally make sense. Let's make-believe
We were destined to fall apart so we could collide again.
It doesn't matter if it's true or not; just tell me it's not over yet.
Tell me you love me. Tell me when I can open my eyes.

happiness is a poem I have yet to write

How am I supposed to tell you that I'm happy now but I'm still scared
You'll kiss me when my lips are sunburnt shoulders, that
I'll flinch away at the slightest touch because
It hurts? I'm scared it'll hurt. I'm scared
You'll hurt me. I'm scared this'll end.
The truth is that I don't know how to be happy and unafraid;
I don't know how to love without the fear of loss
Gnawing at my bones like an animal hungry for its dinner.

I say my heart is happy and that's the truth,
But the wolves can still smell my fear;
This is happiness mixed with being terrified,
This is a paradox, this is a riddle I can't solve
With just your love and my bare hands.
This is my smile that you've burned into your retinas and
My laughter that echoes in your mind long after
The phone line has gone silent and the only place
Where my voice still lingers is inside your head.

I'm still too scared to tell you how badly
I want to take your hands and hold them tightly in mine
Until they've rooted themselves so deep that
I'll never have to let go.
You have a forest growing in your marrow and
I could spend the rest of forever unwinding the vines
From your bones, wrapping them around my heart instead,
Peeling back the layers of your soul until
There are no more secrets left for you to keep.

Here is a secret I've kept from you:
You're a six-foot hole in the ground that will
Swallow me whole someday. Your arms are my grave;
They are empty for now, but soon, I will be there
For you to bury. You make me feel so alive I could die and God,
What a life this is, loving you like this,
Loving you like there's no other way to breathe, like
You are the only atmosphere I'll ever need.

This love is nothing new. We've been here before, together,
Standing at the edge of this precipice, looking up instead of down,
Laughing at the abyss, saying, "It can't hurt us now."
This time, though, I won't feel like wild animals
Are gnawing at my bones. I will learn how to balance
Happiness with fear. I will unravel the forest in your marrow and
You, in turn, will hold me in arms that feel less and less
Like a six-foot hole and more and more like home;
That will be happiness.

Until then,
This poem will have to do.

soliloquy

Please understand me when I say
I haven't felt this way for a while.
I'm not used to fireflies lighting up my spine;
I'm more familiar with moths and how
They eat away at splintered bones and leave holes
In hearts that are already bruised.

See, I've been taught by past loves that
Love is something that should make you run,
Hide, keep quiet so you won't be found out.
But silent screams become flashing yellow lights and
Yellow lights turn red and red turns into scars
And scars take too long to fade and I am tired.

Love has made me weaker than I was before.
I used to call myself a girl with a matchbox
For a heart and hands made of fire, but
That was before I burned your paper love down.
Now, I am fragile like a thunderstorm cracked
Down the middle. I am fragile like shards of glass.
I am fragile in ways that will leave both of us broken
If you get close enough to touch.

I hope you will try and touch me anyway;
See, this is nothing but a shot in the dark and
I've never had good aim, but I can aim my heart at you,
Just in case you want it. I don't care if I miss;
I have nothing left to lose.

Because this feels like something I almost forgot
How to feel. This feels like spinning in circles
Until you fall down, laughing like sunflowers at noon.
This feels like fireflies in July and
Blue August skies and standing in the middle
Of those Texas-summer storms,
Washing the sunburnt pavement clean,
Dancing in the street like dandelion wishes
Come true.

the invention of the atom bomb

This is a catastrophe waiting to happen. This is a minefield
Disguised as first love. This is nuclear warfare between
My head and my heart and fallout is inevitable but
I've still been thinking about loving you until the very end.

We're just two teenagers figuring out what it means
To love someone with all the gunpowder stored
Inside our battle-scarred chests. We had to make room for
One another, had to learn not to fear the sound of
Heartbeats pounding like bombs dropping in our heads,
But I think I've finally found a way to block out the noise;
I think it's in the way you say you love me, as if
You weren't entirely sure you did before but
Now, you know you do.

Tell me we're going to make it. Tell me my heart isn't
Hiroshima. Tell me this love is not Chernobyl.
I will love you.
I will love you.
I will love you.

love grew here, beneath the trees.

I fell in love again this afternoon without a trace
Of the wasps that used to swarm in the pit of my stomach.
It happened with my head on your chest and your voice
Echoing down my spine; it happened here,
Laying in the late-spring early-summer heat,
Where the minutes slowed for us, where
I said your name as if time would stop at the sound.

I called you this: the warmth of the sun
Wrapped around my shoulders, the sound of trees
Singing us love songs under the breath of the breeze.
I call you heartbeats blossoming into something new;
I call you wildflowers in May and you call me
Stealing kisses in June. You call me bravery
In the midst of a battlefield smothered by crows.
I call you a fear that is almost overcome;
I call you loved, and you say that I am loved, too.

This is the part of the story where I reach for your hand,
Fearlessly. It is here, in the late-spring early-summer heat,
Beneath the bending trees, that I am everything
You ever wanted me to be.

poetry for atheists

This is the Gospel according to my love:

You and I are worlds apart but I promise you
One day, I will give you something to worship.
I will make you feel something you have never felt
Before. I will lay beside you in the dark and say
This is my body, given for you; take it from me.

I will write scripture between the shallows of
Your collarbones and the edge of your jaw,
Turn your body into psalms, skin on skin,
Ashes to ashes, dust to dust; I will brush my lips
Against yours like a hymnal page and God,
We'll be so beautiful even Heaven will envy us.

I will give you something holy, something that will leave
Your knees bruising on your bedroom floor.
You'll be praying to a God you don't believe in and
I'll be leaving sacrifices in your sheets.

Your arms are my sacred ground;
Cathedral halls hold no place for me.

how to play with fire

1. I warned you; I told you I was dangerous,
Flammable, easily caught afire, not quite so easily
Put out. You came closer, reached out
To let my flames singe the tips
Of your fingers; I withdrew instead. I said,
I don't want to hurt you but it might end up that way.
You said, please stay.

2. Soon after that you struck a match and
My heart was set ablaze; I was already burning but
Not like this, no, not like this,
Never before like this.

3. We've survived our fair share of rainstorms and
Hurricanes, trying to douse the flames, trying
To change our minds. We've burned this place down
Too many times. We've been soot and smoke and dying embers but
Somehow, we've always risen
From the ashes.

4. I like to tell the story of how,
When I was eight years old,
I was playing with matches in my closet and
Almost burned the whole house down.
Someday I'll tell stories about the boy
Who had the courage to approach a wildfire
With arms outstretched, saying,
Let me love you, let me hold you, let me
Carry your heart in my hands;
I don't care if it burns me alive.

5. You don't play with fire;
You love it instead.

the eye of the storm

There are parts of my body that you haven't touched and
I wish that would change. I've been telling you this for a while:
My heart is a hurricane ready to destroy this love and
We may not make it to tomorrow.

But today, we'll let ourselves be together, get tangled up
In love and your unmade sheets. We'll be quiet and the storm
Will envy us; we'll make a mess and the flood
Will wash us clean.

Today, the wind is wrapped around us;
We're caught in the eye of this storm,
Surrounded by stillness, lungs heaving, bodies heavy,
Your breath hot on my neck. Today, the hurricane is just a sigh.
The wind is calm. Our pulses are steady.

Today, you can't hear the bad news in my heartbeat but
Tomorrow, when your body is no longer close enough to touch,
When the sun has risen and I am almost gone,
You'll feel it boiling in your blood:

This storm is not over.
The worst has yet to come.

this is how it goes

I. You, shirtless; me, in a baggy t-shirt, wondering
How other girls manage to sleep wearing a push-up bra.
You, fingertips trailing down my spine, gentle I love yous
Conveyed without words; me, vulnerable, exposed, despite
The fact that all my clothes are still on.

II. Pull me close, kiss my neck, kiss my lips, kiss me
Wherever you wish until I say no. Maybe I will. Maybe I won't.

III. My hands, your back, foothills that must be
Felt in order to be learned. My eyes are not enough
To learn the peaks and curves; I'm curious.
Let me closer.

IV. Cheap cologne or your aftershave
Mixed with sweat and the faded scent of my shampoo;
Breathe it in. Breathe it in.

V. I'm not terrified of this anymore.

prometheus

I'll show you flame. I'll teach you to burn.
Just tell me when you're ready and I'll light a fire
In your matchstick bones. I will bring a heat
To your soul that you never knew existed
Before. It will rival your warmth. We will burn,
Together, and we will be beautiful while we last.

From the very start I warned you:
I'm just looking for a reason to burn, a love
To wreck, a boy to call my home so I can
Burn the whole place down. It hurts to be caught
Aflame but it's a beautiful kind of pain and
When it ends, it ends in fireworks, in an explosions
That will rattle your bones.

We were made to turn forest fires into love and
Love into poetry and poetry into eternal life;
I'll keep you alive. I'll keep us burning.
This doesn't have to end quite yet.
I was made to be your funeral pyre but
I'm not finished with loving you and
You're not ready to die.

This is what I mean when I call your heart my own.
This is how I breathe through the rising smoke:
Cover my mouth with your lips and
Hope for the best. We will burn,
Together;

I don't care if it kills me.

#2

matchbox girls are the ones who get hurt.

my parasitic lover

My blood must smell sweet to you;
I remember laughing when you said
Mosquitoes must love me as much as you do,
The way they eat me alive and still
Beg for more. I say, you must love the misery
They put me through;
You say, I'm in love with you.

The love you speak of is stagnant, shallow,
Disaster's breeding ground, where the mosquitoes
Go to fuck. I remember standing in the water
When you said, this is the place where
If you're not careful enough,
We'll love too hard and be itching for each other
In the morning.

You know me; I scratch until I bleed.

I remember bruised knees, scraped elbows,
Scars on wrists and ankles and my poetry;
I remember feeling like the blood in my veins
Belonged to you,
My parasitic lover, but you left me flea-bitten,
Itching for your hands, scratching my heart open,
Skin, broken, raw.

RE: future

I had never thought of my ribs as a prison until
My heart decided to try to pound its way out of my chest.
Suddenly, I was no longer responsible for the blood in my veins;
After all, my pulse still sounds like your name, and
Even if it's just my imagination running wild or
The romantic hiding underneath my skin getting the best of me,
It must say something.
I think it says I am so in love with you that
I've let you into my bloodstream, that you are the sole reason
My heart remembers to beat, that your name
Is my only reminder that my blood runs red, not blue.

I have gotten so used to being scared that I have forgotten
How it feels to be unafraid. I have never been brave;
What I feel now is not bravery. This is not the absence of fear,
This is not fearlessness, this is me
Being so in love with you that nothing but you can hurt me.
And I'm telling you I am nothing to love;
I am just a girl with a fierce heart and
Silver-blue eyes that cry a little bit too much.
I have no doubts that I love you more than
You could ever love me,
But here you are anyway.

I have come too far to turn back around now, and
This might end again with a whimper instead of a howl,
But my love is still too fierce to be caged behind ivory bars.
Bravery is different from recklessness, and if there is a God,
He knows I am neither. I am wild instead; I start fist fights
Inside my ribcage, between my heart and my mind, and
I have the teeth of a wolf but I still bite my fingernails smooth.
You don't know what you're getting yourself into;
Our future is ninety percent set in stone but
Mountains still crumble under the weight of the sky and
It takes steel to keep my heart from breaking.

kiss the fear out of me

I still want your lips on my neck and my hands
Around your heart but I don't want to break
Into your ribcage again without your permission.
I made quite a mess the last time I walked in just to
Steal your heart to keep for myself; I left behind
Graffiti of my name and dark black ink stains and
I know I've been careless with your love before
But I promise to be gentle this time if
You'll just be gentle with me.

See, we've each perfected the art of pretending
We didn't break each other's hearts but
I haven't forgotten what it feels like to be carved in two.

You've always been the indestructible one and I'm still wrapped in
Gauze and cellophane and now I'm on fire but that doesn't mean
I am not afraid. I'm ablaze but don't let that make you think
I'm not still all broken glass and no soft edges.
I will cut you open if you don't know where to touch.

Be careful, love, because this love still isn't as fearless
As you'd like for it to be. So kiss me while telling me
I'm not as shattered as I like to make you think,
Even if you're cutting your lips on my sharp corners until your mouth
Tastes like blood. Kiss me like you don't have to clean up
The messes I always leave behind. Kiss me
Like you've always been mine. Kiss me like that will never change.
Remember: we have always healed ourselves just to be
Carved in two again. Remember: I once broke into your ribcage
To steal your heart but this time, I didn't have to.

See, we've each perfected the art of pretending
We didn't break each other's hearts and
I still haven't forgotten what it feels like to be carved in two,
But you can still kiss me until I'm not scared of loving you.

before it's too late

You're promising we'll make it to the end with
That half-full smile on your lips but I can almost hear the words
Echoing off the walls of your half-empty heart.
I'm starting to think you don't mean the things you say.
I'm starting to think you only stay because
You don't want my blood on your hands.
You say you would've left a long time ago if you didn't believe
I could get better, but I'm starting to think
You're more scared of post-midnight phone calls
Than you are of losing me.

I can tell your love is fading fast. I can tell
You're not going to be around much longer.
I'm pretending not to love you as much as I really do
Just in case I get hurt, just in case
You forget to give my heart back before you go;
I've learned it's better to be safe than sorry, and
I'm always the one apologizing.

I'll drop my masquerade when you stop pretending everything's okay.
Until then, I'll be breaking my own heart so you don't have to.

Leave me now while I'm scribbling
Your name on the backs of old receipts,
Leave before I run out of ink, leave
Before you run out of patience.
You don't understand;
I'm a violent ending playing dress-up as forever but
What's the point in forever when we both know
It won't last?

Tell me one more time that it doesn't have to be this way.
Look me in the eye before it's too late.

ghost towns

I've been naming ghost towns after all the things you left behind.
This one is called "My Heart," and its skeletal remains
Have been white-washed by the sun. Main Street
Is dusty and cracked down the middle; the old café
Has cobwebs in the back corners. All the tables are broken.

The houses in "The Only Place I Could Ever Call Home" are empty.
The doors are falling off their rusty hinges. The windows are
All boarded up. Inside, the curtains are moth-eaten and grey and
The paint is peeling off the walls. The sidewalks have dandelions
Growing in-between their split seams; it seems nuclear fallout
Is enough to make you turn away, but it still won't
Convince my hope to get up and leave.

As the dust settled, as you walked out my door,
I vowed that "Memories" would never fall into disrepair;
Now there are broken-down automobiles abandoned on the side
Of the road. They were once on their way to somewhere called
"My Future With You," but all the exit signs on the highway
Have been taken down.

I call this one "Goodbyes Never Spoken."
This one, "Summer." This one, "Our Love."
This one, I named after myself.
I've been turning into a ghost town these days;
The walls of my heart are starting to cave in.

When the dust settles,
I'll name this one after you.

one-third girl and two-thirds mess

Your hands were gripping my throat and your fingers were
Somehow wrapped around my lungs and your arms
Had my heart in a chokehold and you were saying please,
Don't leave, don't go, but I guess you didn't know
I'm one-third human and the rest of me is a mess.
Messes don't plead with you to let them breathe,
They don't beg for mercy, they only ask to be cleaned
From the inside out, and
I told you I was leaving but I'm two-thirds mess
And one-third girl and wholly in love with you.

I told you I was better off on my own but the truth is that
Messes can't clean up the messes they leave behind.
Their fingers wrap around your lungs and their hands end up
Gripping your throat and somehow they make a mess
Of your heart but still you end up asking them to stay because
You're one-third human and the rest of you is something too in love
To let them go.

You were begging me to stay and
I was begging you to make me clean;
Now look at this wonderful mess we've made.
You're two-thirds too in love to let me go and
I'm two-thirds too messy to leave this way and
We're both one-third too human to do anything but stay.

the long road home

You've become something I can't quite name
Off the tip of my tongue. I don't remember much,
But I remember you're something like
Warmth and a heartbeat and the only one
Who can stop me from shaking in my own skin.
You're something like home and
If I had known that the doors weren't locked,
I wouldn't have stayed out in the cold.

I was prepared for another burnout ending,
Another faded reprise of the same tragedy we've had
Every time before.
We've been down this road a hundred times;
I only know how to love and how to run, but
You know how to make me stay.

I know I haven't been easy. I know
I've spat out words like daggers or
Freezing rain and I've picked fights
Just so I could feel something and
I've said sorry too much after
Pointing out your mistakes even though I hate
When you're the one apologizing. I know that
Sometimes, I'm still bitter about you leaving.
I know I'm the only one who doesn't know
How to stay. I know I've run away
Too many times to count and I know
It's a long road back to you now
But I'm coming home.

I'm coming home.

my inkstained hands hold more truth than blood-sealed oaths do

This I vow:

You will never see my hands weave cobwebs.
I don't have spider's legs for fingers;
I am not as delicate. My bones don't break quite so easily.
There's no silk under my fingernails, only dirt;
If you search for frailty, you'll fail.

But someday, I might come home to you with ink-stained fingers and
Paint-splattered hands and I won't realize
How big of a mess I've made of myself.
You'll tell me to smile as you wet your thumb to wipe
A drop of blue off my cheek, and you'll carry me to the bathroom so
I don't collapse onto the floor again.

My bones have never broken and my fingers
Are stronger than they seem but sometimes
I will need reminding that for as long as you've held my hand,
You have never seen me weave spiderwebs.
Tell me how as you washed the ink from my skin,
You didn't find any silk underneath my bitten fingernails;
You only found dirt and that it's all gone now.

I'll glance down at my hands that have never woven a single cobweb
But have tangled themselves into your hands so many times that
I have forgotten what it feels like to not be intertwined with you, and
Then I will find myself triple-knotting my fingers together with yours.
I won't let go.

bloodied knuckles

I get into fist-fights with my mind, throwing punches
When it tells me I'm smarter than this, that
I know better than this, that
You are not worth the wait if I'm the only one waiting.
I was born with a supernova in my veins, it says, and
Loving you will put the fires out, but still I lash out
With my bare hands, bloodied knuckles,
Leaving bruises on my common sense.

My heart knows better, I say. My mind knows nothing
Of what it is like to love during a cease-fire;
It feels like a fight, but all you can do is stand still.
My heart is the scarred one, I scream,
Because my mind has been played with,
But my heart has been beaten black and blue.
My heart can take care of itself just fine, I whisper,
Trying to fool myself into believing that battle scars
Disappear just as easily as razor blade cuts do, but
My mind remains unconvinced. Smiling through tears
Never tricked me into thinking I was happy;

What makes me think lying through broken teeth
Will be any different?

So I throw another punch, the way you once showed me,
Thumb on the outside of my fist instead of tucked in.
"You'll break your hand if you do it that way,"
You said. "You'll break my heart if you leave,"
I whispered. You didn't hear me;
Maybe our hearts were pounding too loud.

But my head has my heart pinned to the ground and
My heart seems to be losing this wrestling match. My head
Is only bruised but my heart is bleeding,
Slashed open by the thought that this will be
Just another stupid mistake. But I swear through split lips that
I was born with a supernova in my veins, and loving you
Only makes it burn brighter. I swear with my bitter tongue that my blood
Is mixed with stardust; maybe that's why your love
Keeps me fighting. Maybe that's why my knuckles shimmer
When they bleed.

monster in the mirror

I can't keep the beasts inside my head. They're crawling
Down my spine, clawing their way into my heart,
Making my chest cavity into a lions' den.
They are making too much noise; I can hear them roaring
In my lungs, warning you: we are carnivores.
We are dangerous. We will hurt you.

The monsters are on the prowl,
Searching for something to devour whole.
You could be an easy kill;
Instead, you stand there, unafraid.
I know my reflection is glinting in your fearless eyes but
I am terrified of seeing the remnants
Of the last thing I ripped apart.
It was an ugly mess, a rotting carcass picked clean, and
I don't want you to see me that way again, with
Salt-stained cheeks and dried blood beneath my fingernails.

Before, I called myself destruction, chaos,
Broken-boned creature in the dead of night.
That was then; now, I am scared and small,
Cowering in fear of what I might become.

So prove to me I'm not a monster. Prove to me that
I am not dangerous. Prove to me that my heart
Is not blackened by the beasts
Who have made themselves at home.

white noise

Listen:
There is too much white noise in this love.

You say my laugh is still stuck in your head and
It has you smiling when you least expect it,
But your voice has been slipping through my fingertips
Since the day you walked out my front door without a word.
I'm sorry, but I can no longer hold your face clearly
In my mind. It's been like that for a while now.
You've been gone too long.

But if you like, I'll let you keep my heart;
Just promise me you'll ignore it when it starts pounding
The sound of your name.
I don't want you to know how much I need you.
I don't want you to know that you still haven't been flushed
From my bloodstream.
Be still, my beating heart; silence is a virtue.

When all has grown quiet, when
My pulse has stilled, when your hands are covered in blood
That is not your own, that is when I ask for you to
Cut me open. It's not like you haven't done it
Dozens of times before. You're awfully good at it now.
You'll perform the autopsy in no time.

Cause of death: asphyxiation. Cause of death:
Too much air, not enough words to fill it up. Cause of death:
Suffocation by white noise. Choking on all the things
I was never brave enough to say. Cause of death:
I held my breath for you too long.

Cause of death: silence.

holy wars

Hope is a thing with claws and I would shred this world to pieces
Just to see you again but you don't seem to need me
Quite the same way I need you. I'm used to you telling me the truth but
It doesn't feel like the truth anymore; it feels like a gunshot wound to the heart.
Your bullets are leaving gaps between my teeth and
All I want is to tell you that I love you but I can't get the words out
Through the sound of you shooting me down.

You have broken me so many times that I think
I have started mistaking my brokenness for something else.
My heart doesn't feel shattered; it feels heavy. It feels tired.
But maybe that's just because broken hearts weigh more
Than whole ones do. Either way, I shouldn't be so tired of loving you.

I've been hoping to meet you again somewhere in-between
The place we turned into holy ground and the battlefields
We've been fighting our holy wars on but God,
I don't think I can do this anymore.
I would fight my way to the end but I don't think I have it in me;
I don't think I can keep fighting if we're not fighting for the same thing.
We've found ourselves on opposite sides of this battleground and
I think I'm done.

This is a ceasefire. This is a surrender. This is white flags raised like warning signs.
White flags like bandages. White flags soaked red.

Someday I will meet you in-between the future and the place
Where my dreams of you go to die. I know you are just
An empty space beating slightly off-center in my chest that
I can't quite fill but God, this exorcism isn't working.
It isn't working. It isn't working. It isn't working.

My hope has caught the plague;
This graveyard is full.

you were never here

I'm a fire escape, not an exit sign
Yet you still say my name like a warning siren shrill on your tongue.
Goodnight could quite easily become a goodbye and
If you add just one word to three it changes the meaning entirely;
Am I just a precaution? Am I only here
Because I make you feel safe? Do you think I'll stay?
Tell me, what will you do when your empty paper house catches fire and
I'm not there with my loving arms to carry you to safety?
Here's the catch: the safety isn't on my gun.
You're staring down the barrel and my finger is on the trigger.

Didn't you know how dangerous it is to play outside in a thunderstorm?
It's not my fault you got struck by lightning;
I warned you. I told you to go back inside to your
Lonely home. I'm starting to think that you'll never listen;
That's okay. I'm not planning on chasing after you anymore.
It's not worth it; my words only get dirty in the dust you leave behind, and
The heavy silence just gets stuck in my throat,
Refusing to sink like a stone the way it should.

You had me tangled up in your grip,
Tossing and turning under unmade bedsheets that have always been
Empty of you. I had dreams where I kissed you,
But in them you were a dark spot from staring directly into the sun
For too long. Your voice is a riddle I've been trying to solve, but
I guess I'm just going to have to start telling myself that
You were never here.
It's not so much a lie as it is a broken promise, and God knows
You've given me so many of those that
I can hardly hold all of the pieces in my empty hands.

This is an ending.
This is me saying I've had enough of being lonely
Instead of being loved. It's about time I let go of your ghost;
It isn't good for anything, anyway, and it doesn't pay its rent.
This is an exorcism. This is me telling you
I'm tired of this gaping hole in my chest that
Some would have the audacity to call a heart. This is me telling you
I'm tired of always being here
When you are not. I walked past your old house a few days ago;
You were never there. You are gone, and I'm telling you, this is it.
This is over. This is done.

don't come looking for me

Come looking for me and you'll lose yourself instead, see,
I'm the one who showed you what it was like to love.
I gave you a box of matches and said, here, take these and
Set yourself on fire; you'll be okay. I've done it
A million times already and I haven't burned to the ground.
I said, this won't be the death of you. I said,
Don't worry; it's me who's going to get hurt.

Come looking for me and you'll just get lost because
This time, I'll be nowhere to be found.
I've learned that some fires aren't meant to burn forever and
The greatest loves are the ones that leave third-degree burns
When their flames are touched; that is what we were.

This is what we are now: a matchbox girl and a boy with a paper heart,
Both burned, both hurting, both tired of trying to control fire.
I've been pressing the backs of my hands to the walls,
But this time, I'm not gone. I'm not leaving.
I'm just putting out the flames.

lipstick stains

You said my name like it was a sunset
Melting on your tongue, like it was your favorite color,
Like it was a lyric from your favorite song, like
If you could only say it enough it would catch on fire and
Ignite the dark matter between us, bring the distance to its knees.
I was a blue-eyed disaster zone, convinced that
Love was only out there to hurt me, that the ten-story fall and
The twelve hundred miles were more a curse
Than a blessing, but then you ripped all the band-aids
From my heart and made yourself at home;
How could I not love you?

The truth is that it never happened that way. We never touched
Like you wanted to, and I was too scared to let you any closer.
But this is my love and I saying we are not ready
To let the melting sun go down without a fight. This is my heartbeat
Or the sound of distant drums; you choose. This is my battle cry.
This is the color of my warpaint. This is the color of my lips
When yours meet mine. This is the color I bleed.

It never happened this way, soft and gentle and unspoken.
It never happened with just a brush of our fingertips,
Sparks flying for a split second before turning to soot.
It never happened with the thunder of storm clouds rolling in, with
Red on my lips and stains on your sheets;
It only ever went like this,
With bloodshot eyes, crying, screaming, and
You, calm as ever, the eye of the storm.

It never happened like this and yet
This is how I choose to remember it:
All fire and no embers. All fury and no pain.
Bloodied knuckles and lipstick stains and when you leave,
You'll take the kerosene and the lighter fluid
And all the matches with you.

It never happened the way I wanted it to but it ended like this:
My name still melting like one last sunset
On your tongue, your favorite songs still on my lips,
The bittersweet picture of the color red
All over everything. I am still a blue-eyed disaster zone.
I still brought this love to its knees. I am the ten-story fall
Still torn between being a blessing and a curse, but
Unlike the dark matter that unraveled at its seams,
Your heart will never come clean of me.

#3

matchbox girls rise from their ashes.

creationism

I.
In the beginning, something happened:

An explosion in my chest, the sound of every atom in my body
Colliding with one another at the speed of light, my heart crashing
Into my ribcage, my lungs; it was a crime scene. It was a birth.
They say that within three seconds, everything the universe needed
For it to become was already there. All I know is something happened.
I don't know what to call it; the closest I can come to a descriptor
Is your name.

This is how I was created: you, a boy with strong arms and gentle hands,
As if you had shouldered the universe for so long that it taught you
How to love a girl with nebulae in her bloodstream. You took my heart,
Forged stars from my veins, gave them back to me with a look that said
I was more a universe than anything you had ever known. When I asked
Why you chose to love a mess, you replied: the universe is still beautiful
In all its chaos. The universe is still beautiful even when some cataclysm
Tears it apart. It will always fall back together.

II.
I want to know:
Is that why you couldn't stay?

III.
In the end, something happened:

A sharp pain in my chest, the feeling of infinity shattering
Before my eyes, a supernova but without the violent elegance
I always thought we'd be; it was a fallout zone. It was a morgue.
They say that the universe will collapse one day, when it has
Expanded so far that it can no longer hold itself together without
Tearing itself apart. Tell me, is that why my heart has no more room
Left within it for me to love you?

This is how I was destroyed: me, a girl with so much gravity that
She couldn't help but hold onto a boy who didn't want to be
Tethered down. Still I untangled the threads of the universe, rearranged
Entire galaxies for you in hopes that maybe you would look at me again;
I guess you forgot how to carry chaos on your shoulders.
There's this theory that creation is impossible and destruction is
Only the stuff of poetry. I don't know if that's the truth;
All I know is something happened, and the only thing I can call it
Is your name.

I loved you like unpaid bus fare

Last night, I dreamt that I was with you again. I dreamt
We lay in bed the way we never actually did and when I woke up,
Your warmth still lingered between my unmade sheets.
But I didn't ask for this. I didn't ask you to haunt my dreams.
I never asked to wake up from them not knowing
Whether I should laugh at their absurdity or cry at the truth
That they were only in my head. I never asked for this ending.
I never asked to be given a one-way ticket away from your love.
I only ever asked for you to love me the way you used to.

I tell everyone I loved you like unpaid bus fare; I let you into my heart
But you didn't pay for your ticket. I tell everyone I loved you in
Subway glances, moments of happiness flashing by before
Being thrust into darkness again. When I tell everyone the lie of how
You simply got off at the wrong stop, I am told not to look back because
I'm not going that way.

They don't understand how the veins in your arms are a transit map that
Only I know. It leads to the only place I could ever call home, and
Home is your chest. Home is your heartbeat. Home is warmth.
Home is you, and I don't know how to look straight ahead when
The only thing I've ever wanted is what I'm leaving behind.
Turn me into a pillar of salt; I don't care. I know the taste of my tears
Well enough already.

There was a time when we planned the future as if it were only a
Plane ticket away. As if we actually stood a chance. As if we had
All the time in the world and it would never run out. Maybe we were
Too naïve back then; maybe our hopes were set too high.
It doesn't matter. I still can't keep myself from turning around.

You're no good for me, but you used to be;
Please. I just want a return ticket to the way things were before.

color theory

He told me I was red as he watched me bleed and
I pointed to each of the cuts and said,
This is where you hurt me. This is where
You called me red and I wondered why
Your favorite color was still blue. This
Is where you first loved me and where
I fell to your feet, begging you on skinned knees
To love me again.

It wasn't always this way;
He used to be the one who loved more,
Who took me in even when I was nothing but
Bruised elbows and broken bones, who
Held me close and helped me breathe.
He used to be the one who bandaged
My wounds; now he's the one who loves
Less, or not at all. Now he leaves.

He left me for dead, left my heaving lungs
Turning black and blue, left my heart
Cleaved into halves. He didn't bother to cauterize
The wounds or give me needle and thread but
I've counted: I'll need twelve hundred stitches to
Fix myself up again.

But at least with all these scars on my ribs I have proof
Of how I was so in love with him that I let him break my bones,
One by one, piece by piece, until all that was left of me
Was a pulse that could barely stand on its own.

At least with all these bruises
Up and down my heart, I can point to each one and say:
He was here, once. He was here and
I called his abusive hands love. He was here,
Back when the sunsets were still red and
The sky was still blue, back before they dissolved
Into the perfect shade of a purple bruise like
Blood vessels broken beneath my skin, like
I never learned how to leave and he
Never figured out how to stay, like
We were both in love but now,
I'm the only one.

hurts like poetry

I don't write love poems; I write scars.
I write third-degree burns. I write like
Open-heart surgery, like this is going to take
A while to heal, like the blood is clotting but
I'll probably pick the scabs open again tomorrow.

I write poetry like salt in fresh cuts, like
This severs me in two, like
You should have known better,
I should have known better,
One of us should have cauterized the wounds
Before they festered.

If this is love, I don't want it;
It hurts like poetry, like a Caesarian-section birth,
Like you cut me open right down the middle but
Forgot the morphine. It hurts like
Blood everywhere, pain everywhere, and you,
Fleeing from the scene of the crime, gone.

novocaine

Two months have passed and I'm crying for the first time since
The night it ended but there isn't enough oxygen
Left in my lungs for me to make a sound.
I should have screamed before I left you that I loved you
With all two hundred and six bones in my body but instead,
I swallowed the sound and chased it down with
Painkillers and poetry; for you, I kept quiet. For you,
I learned how to hold my tongue. For you, I pretended
Not to feel a damned thing.

The truth is that you feel too little and I feel too much;
Teach me how to be numb, like you, like your warm eyes
Gone cold, like your hands no longer wanting my touch
Imprinted upon your skin. Give me a shot of novocaine so
I'll stop wondering if liquor could replace your lips.
Give me something strong to get me through the night;
I don't want to want the strength in your arms,
But it seems I have no choice.

You said it doesn't have to be this way but
What you don't understand is that loving you taught me
How to keep my hopes for the future locked up
In the medicine cabinet. Loving you taught me to keep
Tally marks on my bathroom floor instead of on my wrists,
Numbering the days since the last time you left,
Counting down until the moment when you'd break my heart
Again. Loving you taught me silence and now,
I don't remember how to scream.

My tears are too quiet but the pain is so loud;
I don't want to feel a damned thing.

bioluminescence

You snapped my spine just to watch me glow and I didn't cry;
I lit up like the Milky Way, one hundred billion scintillating stars,
All for you. I know how to give love in return for love but
When you take your love away, I keep on giving.
I didn't know that this time, you didn't want my heart;
You wanted my light so you could walk away
Without tripping over your lies.

When you took my body into your arms I thought
This is what it must feel like to be a firefly, illuminated
From the inside out, warmth finally reaching from your hands to
My permafrost bones. I never expected things to go as planned but
I was certain of something: you were the one who softened me,
Turned the savage glint in my eyes into starlight you could love.
You were the one who put an electric current in my veins.
You were the one who turned the lights out.
You were the one who broke me in the darkness.

I lost my voice while choking back tears, while you
Systematically took every vertebrae out of its place, as if
You knew I would light up like the Milky Way again.
I couldn't say a thing as light spilled from my fractured bones,
Couldn't tell you that I loved you until I had nothing left of you to lose
And there was nothing left of me for you to break.

I loved you until I found my voice again, in the darkness,
Trying to forget the way you looked into my starry eyes,
Remembering all too well how it all went wrong. It happened like this:
You snapped my spine and I blinded you with the shine
Of an entire galaxy. You snapped my spine and I burned you
With the fire of a thousand suns, saying,
My light is mine. My light is not yours to steal.
My heart is not yours to break.

You snapped my spine just to watch me glow and
I didn't cry;

I screamed.

response to a rhetorical question asked on the sixty-fourth day

You ask me "what do you want" as if you expect my response
To be anything other than what you are used to, as if
You honestly believe there will be a different answer
This time around, as if there is something wrong with wanting something,
As if there is something wrong with wanting you, and
Maybe you're right; maybe there is nothing left within you
For me to love. Maybe it was a mistake to call you when I knew
The dial tone would run out before you managed to
Pick up the phone, but maybe it was also a mistake for you to say
It was all just some pathetic heartbeat you wanted to erase.
Maybe it was a mistake for you to let me leave. Maybe
It was a mistake for you to let me go. It doesn't matter.

This is what I want: your love. Not the generic kind.
If I wanted it over-the-counter I would walk to the drugstore
Half a block down from your old street. If I wanted something cheap
I would get some aspirin, something to keep my heart
From hurting as much, but I think by this hour the pharmacy is closed.

If you thought you'd get a different answer this time around, you were wrong.
I want you, just as I always have, but if that's too much to ask
I will settle for pretending that your love was never mine to call home.
I will pretend that you never gave your heartbeat to me, not even once,
Even though you offered it so many times I lost count.
Maybe that's the problem; instead of monitoring your pulse,
I kept tally marks of how many days had passed
Since the last time you took it away.

You're not giving it back now, I know that, and I won't make you.
It's your love, after all, and I only could only take up residence
In its hallways for so long. Maybe I left all the lights on. Maybe
I ran up the bills. Maybe I forgot to pay my rent a few times.
In any case, I will make up a world in my head where
We were happy, once, together, and I will live the lie that
We are happy, now, apart.

This is what I want: happiness, preferably in the shape of your smile or
In the warmth of your body or in the strength of your shoulders and back,
But I understand that none of those things are mine to call home now.
I understand that your hands are probably itching for someone new
To hold, someone closer, someone stronger, someone
Easier to love, and I understand that I am none of those things.
I understand that I am nothing to you and that by now,
You should be nothing to me. That's okay. I've seen your heart;
There is nothing left within it of what I want.
But at the very least, I want to know that
I can be happy,
Here,
Alone.

voicemail for the 9-1-1 operator

At the scene of the crime I was crying,
Collapsed, shaking on my bed and you
Were already gone again, leaving with my heart
Again, clutched, bleeding in your hands;
See, I thought I had rid myself of you but
I guess I'll just be more careful
With changing the locks next time.

You, the burglar, the thief, the criminal
Who gets a thrill out of midnight car chases,
The sound of sirens shrieking in the night
Blurred with tears and blood;
You, the boy, the man whose voice
I could not recall even if I wanted to,
Whose face will not be on WANTED posters
Because I don't remember it:
Get out. Get out. I don't want you on these streets.
I don't want you in this home.

This was a hit-and-run, this was
You decided to break all my windows in because
The doors were locked, this was
I hope you know what you've done;
You've stolen something valuable of mine and
I want it back. I want you gone.

ghost story

This is a ghost story,
Not the scary kind,
Just the sort of corpse-skinned memory that
Passes through walls and
Fades in and out of dreams:

It is half-past midnight and my heart
Has missed its curfew once again.
I don't want to go home because
Home is empty and the floorboards creak and
There's a moaning in the rafters that sounds
An awful lot like you and
I feel like a ghost in my own bed.

I should be haunting you instead of
The other way around, but the truth is
This house feels like a rotting corpse.
This house smells like blood tastes,
Bitter with a bite and a pair of claws.
This house is rotting with all the desire
Of lovers making love;
It is swallowing whole the memories
In the corridors and the poetry
Slashed into the walls and
I am being devoured heart-first with the rest of it.

You see,
I paced around the church graveyard on the day
Of our love's funeral, asking God
To let us rest in peace this time, but I don't know
If he heard me. Lately, I have been wondering
Whether six feet was enough to bury our love
Or if I should've asked you to dig us
A deeper grave. I've also been thinking
Of shedding my skin;
I have this theory that if I become nothing
But a pile of bones, your ghost will go away.

Someone always loves more, I know that,
But I wasn't warned that the one who loves less
Is the one who stays.
I thought you would leave
And take your shadows with you,
But instead they've taken up residence
In the cobwebbed corners of our old haunts and
This exorcism isn't working and
I don't know how to get rid of you the way
You got rid of me.

I've cleaned up the mess
You left behind, all the dust and
Caved-in ceilings and broken glass,
But this house still feels like a rotting corpse.
This house still smells like blood tastes,
Except now my wounds have festered and
The scent of blood has gone stale.
This house is still haunted and it still
Does not feel like home.

Please, tell your ghost to leave me alone.
I don't want it anymore.

labyrinth

We were wandering dirt paths overgrown with green and
I was memorizing your footsteps backwards because
I've never been good at telling my left from my right but
In the case of your departure, I wanted to know how to get back
To the way things were before.

It turns out I ended up memorizing you instead, the way your arms
Were stronger than anything I'd ever known before but still
Careful not to break me in two, the way your brown-sugar eyes
Turned to gold in the sun, the way your pulse knew
Just how much you loved me and pounded its way out of your chest
So that the whole world would know it, too.

I forgot to memorize the way out of this love,
And then you were gone.

See, there was a time when I would've written this poem
Into a list of all the right questions I would ask if only
I were brave enough to hear all the wrong answers. But you left.
You left me and ever since I've been lost because
I don't know these overgrown paths the way
I used to know your hands.

Now I've just been retracing my steps, trying to remember
Our pilgrim's path to holy ground so I can figure out how to
Leave it all behind. It doesn't feel the same with you gone.

I don't know my way around my own heart anymore, but
I'm slowly learning that I never needed you to find me
In order to not feel lost; I only needed to lose you
So I could find myself. I still don't know my left from my right,
But I do know you left me behind and there are no wrong answers
To right questions, only right and wrong ways to leave
After your love has lost its way.

This is the way things were before.

the black death

My heart is tossing and turning in its feverish state but
Somehow, you've managed to get back into it.
I want to get rid of you, a bacterium that spreads,
A wound that festers, the bubonic plague
In human form, but it's no use.

You make me sick to my stomach and now
I'm buckling over in pain trying not to cry over you.
I'm supposed to be over you, remember?
You're not supposed to be a hallucination
In the back booth of a restaurant I haven't set foot in
Since you were here. I thought I was out of the past,
But I'm still seeing it in every flea-bitten corner.

I wanted you to have and to hold,
For better, for worse. I wanted you
In sickness and health,
Not just in poetry that never seems to heal
From its aching.
I should've told you all this, I suppose,
But it's too late to say I love you now.
The plague takes over.

And all you'll do is watch me as beads of sweat form
On my pale skin watch me as my shaken bones splinter,
Watch me as I vomit all the sweet nothings
You ever placed into my naïve head. Watch me as I cough up blood.
Watch me as the world spins and fades and I am purged of you.

Until death do us part.

this is an apology for the way love fades

This is not a eulogy for our love;
Everyone has heard enough about it already.

This is me saying I am sorry for running.
Sorry for leaving. Sorry for loving. Sorry for
Not coming back. This is all the sorries I ever gave,
All the sorries you never said, all the regrets
I still have from losing you.

This is me forgiving you for breaking my heart, for
Each and every hairline crack, for that last low blow,
All my love coming crashing down.
This is me saying I forgive you for everything,
Even the time you said you were just caught up
In emotion and you didn't want that feeling in your chest.
This is my forgiveness. I don't want to hate you.

This is an apology for the minute I stopped loving you;
The hands on the clock are standing still, waiting,
Waiting, waiting. This is an apology for all the waiting
I did for you. This is you, never apologizing
For not waiting for me. This is me, forgiving as I forget.

This is an apology for the way love fades,
For how one moment I loved you and the next,
That love was gone. This is an apology for my hope,
For how I thought we'd burn longer but even flames
Need a little room to breathe. This is an apology for heartbeats
Like dead languages. This is an apology for the way I left,
Wanting you to follow me, disappearing into the distance,
Going, going,
Gone.

memento mori

Reminder: my heart will stop beating someday. Reminder:
This, I already know. It doesn't seem like it's been very long
Since I checked for your pulse and found nothing in its place,
But I suppose the clock doesn't keep ticking once time has run out.

I'm sorry; I simply forgot love is not supposed to last forever.
I should've known your heart would stop beating while my pulse
Still sounded like your name. It's just that my heart is tired.
I think it's about time I let it die in its sleep.

But first, I must thank you for digging my grave. I'm six feet
Underground in a coffin made out of nails and broken promises and
I'm not in pain anymore. I think being buried alive hurt less
Than loving you while your heart was dead ever did.

My love has had its funeral. My love is a rotting corpse,
Skin pulled taut on clean white bones. It was last seen
Wearing its Sunday best, but that was only an apology
For the mess it left behind.

What a shame; I don't think I'm in love anymore.

to the next girlfriend

Falling for him won't be easy.
It will happen in slow-motion or at the speed of light,
But it will never be easy.
It will feel like you're trying to walk underwater,
Sinking like a stone; it will be as if you stepped off
The pockmarked surface of the moon,
Just to fall into the sun. It will take an infinity
Or eight minutes. It will leave you shivering
In the dampness or burning in his atmosphere,
But either way, you better watch where you're going,
Because he'll say he'll catch you but that's something
He doesn't always do.

When he asks if he can call you something else,
Let him. But be careful, because
He has a way of making a name seem like
So much more. Please, be careful;
He might steal your identity in a single breath
When he says your new name aloud for the first time.
When he adds words of love to the end,
The name you were given at birth
Will mean nothing at all. This is your christening;
This is when you will stop believing in God
Because his touch feels like all things holy and
His voice is divine. If you're not careful,
This will be the moment when you lose yourself all at once;
All at once, you will cease to be the creation of a Creator.
You will become the creation of love instead.

Soon enough, you will find your bodies so close
You can hear his heart pounding like a thunderstorm
In his chest. Close your eyes; you'll be blinded by his lightning
If you don't. When he tells you he loves you,
Don't you dare let them flicker open, don't you dare
Let the rain in, don't you dare let those words get to your head
Before they reach your heart. Ask him to repeat them,
Just to be sure, just so you can hear him say the words
A dozen times, maybe more.
Only look at him when you are certain his love letters are true.
Your eyelids are envelopes, sealed with a kiss;
Once you tear them open, your lips are hiss and your eyes
Will never see clearly again.

He'll use invisible ink as he writes his promises
Onto your skin, but you'll still feel the poetry of his love,
Even after his fingertips are gone.
There will come a night when you are unable to fall asleep
Because you'll have realized his warmth
Feels slightly colder, and his body in your bed
Seems further away, and the kisses he places
All over you feel less like poetry and more like an essay
He must finish before dawn. All of a sudden,
There will come a morning where the sun will rise,
Just as it always does, but he won't be looking at you.
This will be the morning he tells you he loves you,
One last time, just another memorized line, just another
Broken promise written on your skin like poetry gone wrong.
Then he will leave you without a second thought.

When it ends,
You will realize you never wished for forever
Until forever ran out.

epilogue

I bet you're kissing other girls now,
Just like I'm falling in love with other boys
For a few seconds at a time;
This is how we erase each other,
By giving our hearts away in smaller pieces
Than we are used to.

We used to trade love songs in hopes that
Someday, we would find a place
Where we could settle down
With our restless hearts cradled in our tired hands.
We used to pass laughter back-and-forth
Like a liquor bottle, drunk on our love,
Wishing for a dark place in the other's chest
To light a fire within and call home.
We used to give our hearts away whole,
But that was before we left each other for
Other girls and other boys and different lives
Where we were never in love,
Just too caught up in emotions
We didn't know how to feel.

Here I am, clinging to the past in the same way
You stare at your phone before deleting
All our texts; see, we never made love.
We never even fucked. We only knew
How to make-believe our love would survive
In a future that was never ours to keep.

Now, we're giving away our hearts in halves,
Thirds, mere fractions of what they used to be. Now,
You're kissing a different girl every week and I'm
Falling in love with a different boy every day.
Now, I know better than to love in full.
Now, you haven't learned your lesson.
You're trying to hollow out the part of your chest
I used to call home, but you can't erase me
Quite as easily as you want to;
We never touched in the way
Two young lovers should.

It's funny; we used to take such good care
Of each other's heartbeats,
And now we can't even tend to our own.

I hope you're kissing other girls now.
I hope you don't love them.

letter to the boy who offered me friendship

I regret to inform you that my heart is still beating, but
Not to the sound of your name. This time, my love
Is softer to the touch, more delicate, less sharp, less
Dangerous to fall into without someone below to catch me.

There's another boy; he's in love with another girl,
Or two, or three, see, he's never completely over
Anyone he falls for. His heart is a crime scene
Wrapped up in caution tape but there aren't any bullets
Stuck between his teeth. There's no trace of barbed wire
On his tongue. He's been broken, bloodied, bruised;
But then again, so have I.

I'm slipping under and I don't know if I'm in deep yet or
If I'm just looking for a way out of you, but I do know
I keep wishing he'll fall for me, softly, not too hard;
We both have hollow bones, and I don't want to break
The echoes we each have locked up inside our chests.

I think I want a love that whispers instead of howling.
I think I just want a love that won't cut me until I bleed.

stellar corpse, stillborn, still burning

It's taken all these months for me to take the nighttime
Into my own hands,
To tear apart my skin just to prove to the stars
I have a supernova in my bloodstream.
I want to show them: I am burning
With the light of a hundred galaxies,
Chasing each other down like Vicodin and rum.
I want to show you: I am playing with matches next to a gas leak
Again, and this time, I'm using less caution. I want to tell you:
All these months,
I have occupied the silence in-between the stellar corpses
Of our love. I have been here far too long,
Picking at my cratered bones,
Wondering where all the dust
Was coming from. Fate gathered all its starlit things
Before it walked away and although
I was much less tidy in my exodus,
The Universe didn't stop me from leaving and
Neither did you.

But after all these months of stillborn nights and
Memories miscarried in my small, shaking hands,
I have occupied this burning silence
Just to say: I miss you.

eclipse

For girls with fire for hair and starry eyes but
Hearts that can be seen straight through:

I bet when he saw you, he thought
You would be an easy kill. I bet
He saw your shadow, saw how frail
It was, didn't know how sharp its edges could be.
You had claws hidden up inside your sweater sleeves
But for him, you were soft. You were tender.
You were kindling for a fire that never burned.

This is where you learn how to walk on eggshells,
How to keep quiet, how to keep your wishes to yourself
Or else they won't come true. This is where
He leaves the first bruise; this is where his voice,
Once your favorite sound, turns bitter.

I bet when you saw him, you thought
He would be different. I bet he made you feel
Like your stomach was filled with wasps;
I bet his touch felt like an electric shock.
That should've been enough warning signs for the night,
But you were curious, wading into the deep end,
Even though he never taught you how to swim, even though
You were guaranteed to drown.

This is where you learn how to dance on your own again.
This is where you take your own heart,
Cover up the bruises, love yourself for all the poetry
Still left within your hollow bones.
This is where you burn with all the fire of the sun.
This is where your shadow cuts deep. This is where his bitterness
No longer creeps in.

I am a force of nature

I have loved you like a hurricane,
With a flooded heart and trembling hands that
Never knew how to carry you to safety.
I have smothered you and drowned your love,
Bending my fragile spine over backwards while
Tying the sky into knots, trying to teach you
How to weather the storm, but you never learned.

I have loved you with dirt beneath my fingernails
From all the canyons I carved into being
With nothing but a chisel and my own heartbeat.
I have loved you with the strength of a river in the spring.
I am stronger than the earth I stand upon;
I am stronger than you, the boy I loved, the boy
Who left me behind, even though I
Was the one who walked away.

I have loved you savagely, ruthlessly,
With all the forces of nature swelling in my bones.
I have risen like a tsunami from these wildfire ashes, see,
Too much love is a curse when you take,
Then give, then take again, but
I have loved you like a seaside wind, an autumn breeze,
Trees shifting, changing, chameleons in the face of winter.

I have loved you like cracking thunder.
I have loved you with broken glass for teeth.
I have been destroyed so many times that
Disaster is my friend and chaos
Is my lover, but
He isn't you.

He'll never be you.

portrait of the artist

I am just a girl made of unsmoked cigarettes,
Stepping over the cracks in the pavement where their last remains
Are buried, untouched nicotine and stainless steel fingers but
God knows my heart is blackened, God knows
My lungs are filled with graphite dust from breathing in too much poetry;

I am just a girl made of fractured bones
That have only ever been broken in poems, just like my heart,
Just like my fingernails, just like the split ends
In my hair, just like my chapped lips, except
Those things are broken beyond repair in real life, too;

I am just a girl made of wolves' teeth and butterfly wings,
Razor-sharp points that have the power to tear you in half and
Delicate creatures that somehow manage to fly away
In the way I have always wanted to,
Despite the fact that my claws weigh me down;

I am just a girl made of walls painted aquamarine and
Plain white guessing-game ceilings
With glow-in-the-dark stars stuck to them;

And see, I am just a girl made of little pieces that never really
Make sense, mismatched plastic Easter eggshells and
Missing halves that got pieced together all wrong,
Colors that don't really go together anymore but once did;

Isn't that beautiful?

index

Before it's too late	30
Bioluminescence	56
Bloodied Knuckles	36
Color Theory	52
Creationism	49
Don't come looking for me	44
Eclipse	74
Epilogue	70
Forever was written on the walls of your mother's kitchen	3
Ghost Story	61
Ghost Towns	32
Happiness is a poem I have yet to write	11
Holy Wars	40
How to play with fire	18
Hurricane Red	4
Hurts like poetry	54
I am a force of nature	75
I loved you like unpaid bus fare	51
Icarus Falling	9
Kiss the fear out of me	28
Labyrinth	63
Letter to the boy who offered me friendship	72
Lipstick Stains	45
Love grew here, beneath the trees	16
Love poems written in Braille	10
Matchbox Girl	8

Memento mori	67
Monster in the mirror	38
My inkstained hands hold more truth than blood-sealed oaths do	35
My parasitic lover	25
Novocaine	55
One-third girl and two-thirds mess	33
Poetry for atheists	17
Portrait of the artist	76
Prometheus	22
Racing Hearts	7
RE: Future	26
Response to a rhetorical question asked on the sixty-fourth day	58
Sharp-toothed love	5
Soliloquy	13
Stellar corpse, stillborn, still burning	73
The Black Death	65
The eye of the storm	20
The invention of the atom bomb	15
The long road home	34
This is an apology for the way love fades	66
This is how it goes	21
To the next girlfriend	68
Voicemail for the 9-1-1 operator	60
White Noise	39
Wild Thing	6
You were never here	42

acknowledgements

Matchbox Girl was quite a journey. I had my fair share of difficulties in its creation, not to mention I nearly gave up on the project entirely, but I had so many supporters along the way who kept me going, even when I desperately wanted to quit. This is the part of the book where I get to thank all of them.

First, I want to thank my parents for never telling me that it was stupid to want to be a writer when I grew up and for always being my number one fans despite the fact that they haven't read any of my writing since I was eleven years old. You guys can read this one.

Thank you to Ethan Goldstein for being my best friend for as long as I can remember. My life would not be the same without you.

There are two people whose advice and friendship were critical throughout this whole process, so they get a whole paragraph to themselves. I would like to thank Sean Glatch for all the brutally honest critiques and also for reblogging all my stuff on Tumblr. It's debatable which was more helpful in the creation of *Matchbox Girl*. Additionally, a huge thank you goes to Rachel Schmieder-Gropen for having conversations in all-caps with me and finding flaws in even my best poetry, despite the fact that you almost always disagreed with Sean's critiques. Combined, you and Sean are the reason the majority of these poems are worthy of publication, but seriously, you guys need to find something to agree on for once.

Thank you to all my other writer friends, past and present, who are too many in number to be listed here, as well as the entire Teenage Poets Society on Facebook.

Thank you to all my former teachers and mentors who encouraged me to write. All of you will get autographed copies, as promised so many years ago.

I definitely want to thank my friends and followers on Instagram for being just as excited for this as I was. You guys watched *Matchbox Girl* go from a New Year's resolution to a physical book with real pages and a cover that got redesigned like three and a half times. This journey would not have been the same without your support.

Lastly, I want to thank seven-year-old Rachel Sandene for dreaming of being a published author someday. I know you wanted to be a novelist, not a poet, but I promise we'll get there once I manage to actually finish a novel. I want you to know that your words are important, no matter who they're written for. I want you to know that you make beautiful things. Your dreams are the reason why I'm now a published author and *Matchbox Girl* exists. Hopefully this is just the first of many beautiful things we'll make.

about the author

Rachel Sandene is a nineteen-year-old writer and visual artist who feels the world too deeply. Her favorite things are creativity, outer space, Taylor Swift, and the color aquamarine. She currently attends the Savannah College of Art and Design, where she is studying illustration and creative writing. Her superpower is her effervescence. Matchbox Girl is her first published work.

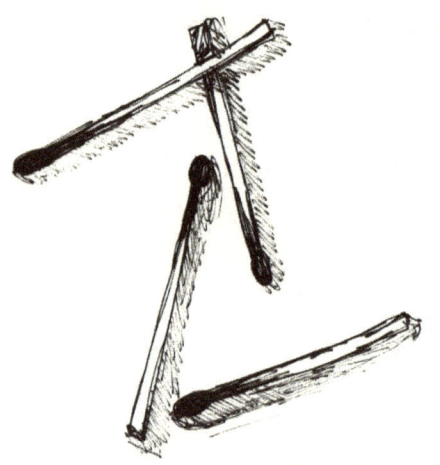

www.ingramcontent.com/pod-product-compliance
Lightning Source LLC
LaVergne TN
LVHW091316080426
835510LV00007B/514